MESSAGES OF
GRACE

111 NOTES OF LOVE
AND GUIDANCE
FROM YOUR ANGELS

ANNA GRACE TAYLOR

For more information, info@annagracetaylor.com.

First paperback edition November 2020

Cover design by Samantha Winstanley

www.annagracetaylor.com

For my Grandma, Elizabeth Grace

Praise for Anna Grace Taylor

"Anna has certainly found her Calling – to bring the healing light of the Angels into the everyday. This book is an essential tool for receiving instant, clear guidance from the angelic realm. One to cherish at home, and keep with you on-the-go!"

Sophie Bashford, Hay House author of You Are a Goddess

"Anna Grace Taylor's messages from the angels have been comforting me for so many years now that I have lost count. With 111 Messages of Grace, Anna brings together the true gold of the angelic treasure that she has been accumulating for so long. Whatever worries or challenges exist in your life, the angels have guidance for you and Anna has followed her Divine life purpose to bring their loving words to you through this book.

I have often said that Anna has, 'the voice of an angel.' I meant her singing voice, but this book shows that it's also true to say that she is 'a voice for the angels.' She is their scribe and angelic translator. 111 Messages of Grace puts that knowledge right in your hands."

Radleigh Valentine, best-selling Hay House author and spiritual teacher

Acknowledgements

The idea for this book was birthed during a lockdown but has been a long time coming, and I'm deeply grateful to so many who have made it possible, especially:

My Angels and Guides – thank you for reminding me why I'm here, for teaching me that anything is possible and for the love that goes beyond all words.

Andrea Zonn and Jo Beth Young – thank you for being the hearts that understand me, the voices that soothe me and the artists that inspire and encourage me. You are golden, and I would not have done this without your incredible love and friendship. I adore you.

Cat Knott and Emma Holmes – thank you for helping me do what I do and for transforming my business and life. You are such a blessing.

Anna Jordan, Athena Groumoutis, Carol Raab, Dawn Evanko, Donna Jenkins, Friday Ng, Helen Barry, Heather Hildebrand, Jilly Wootton, Judy Porter, Justin Roberge, Karen O'Connor, Laura Chelmick, Meg Haines, Polly Ford, Radleigh Valentine and Sophie Bashford – thank you for believing in me the way you do. You are all beautiful people.

To all my other friends, too many to mention by name. You know who you are – thank you for all your love, laughter and prayers.

Mojo Prowse – thank you for all your great feedback, proof-reading and editing. You have been so very helpful and patient.

Samantha Winstanley – thank you for your vision and artistry and for making my book look so pretty.

My gorgeous nieces and nephews – thank you for filling my heart with so much joy. You are the lights of my life.

To the rest of my family, especially Mum and Dad, Karen, Jim and Tom – thank you for giving me strong roots and the freedom to fly in my own direction. I love you all very much.

And finally, to my beloved social media followers and clients; anyone who has ever attended my Angel Afternoons, all the students of my Angelic Connection Course and the wonderful members of my Angel Academy – thank you for all we've shared and for trusting me.

Introduction

Lying on the bathroom floor, I remember saying a silent prayer:

'Please, someone help me. There must be more to my life than this.'

I was twenty years old and had been chronically ill for almost all my teenage years. My parents' marriage was also ending, my twin sister and closest friends had just left home for university, and I was physically and emotionally shattered. I could not study. I could not work. At my worst, having a shower was a massive effort. I felt betrayed by my own body.

Now, as I tried so hard to control something, in the midst of such uncertainty, I found myself with a crippling obsessive, compulsive night-time routine that would often keep me awake for hours. I had never felt so anxious and exhausted in my life. On that particular night, I was beginning to reach my limit when I unexpectedly heard a voice rise up within me.

'I am right here. Keep going. You know who you are and you will help many.'

I felt myself take a deep breath and climbed into bed.

Nothing changed immediately, but just a few weeks later, I won a competition to see the singer Robbie Williams perform his latest single for a TV show in London. I was a big fan and so excited at the opportunity to see him again, especially as it meant my sister would come home for the weekend to go with me.

A lovely nurse at the studio became my Angel that day when she saw my wheelchair and asked me a few questions for the purpose of fire safety. I briefly shared my challenges, and in response, she told me she had asked Robbie to come and say hello.

That moment when he held my hand was a miracle for me. The energy I felt in our exchange, the care, the joy, the gratitude truly lifted my heart when I needed it most.

Later that night, I went to bed much easier, and in my half-awake, half-asleep state, I suddenly saw a huge golden-pink light fill my bedroom. It was both bright and gentle; soft yet completely present. The love and peace that enveloped me were indescribable and profound. It probably only lasted a few seconds, but it was as if time stood still and I knew I had just seen an Angel.

So let me say this: while I would never wish to repeat my pain, and I don't believe I had to suffer to grow, I have come to understand that many of us experience that literal or metaphorical 'moment on the bathroom floor' in order to see that there is, indeed, more to life.

I don't just believe in Angels; I know they exist. Because I have felt that same love; I have seen that light and heard that voice over and over again. It has comforted and supported me, and the thousands of clients I've since worked with, in a multitude of ways – including through messages like the ones you'll find in this book.

In every message, they share guidance on various things – your purpose, your fear, your joy, your relationships, your creativity, your strength, your light, your grief – but they all have one thing in common: they always, always end with a reminder of their love.

The Angels are love. Whether you believe in them or not, they believe in you. Whether you see them or not, they see you. They are unconditionally loving, non-denominational beings here to help you with anything and everything whenever you ask.

It is my fervent hope that the messages on these pages serve as a reminder of that, whatever you're going through.

How to Use This Book

It is my intention that this book is used as an oracle. Any time you need guidance, you can ask the Angels to bring you a message through it. All you have to do is hold the book in your hands, close your eyes, take a deep breath and spend a moment in quiet. Then you might say something simple like:

'Thank you, Angels, for sending me a message through this book. Thank you for sharing with me what I most need to know right now.'

Open it at random and trust that whatever page you turn to is what is meant for you. Or instead, you can ask the Angels to give you a number from 1 – 111. Pay attention to whatever number comes to mind first and then find that number in the book.

Try it now and see what happens. You can't make a mistake. If you have this book, you are already being guided. I have included a blank page after each message for you to journal your thoughts.

In amongst the messages, you will find Angel prayers, poems and affirmations to support you.

I've also created a free audio meditation to enhance your connection with the book and your Angels. To download your copy, visit:

annagracetaylor.com/messagesofgrace

May you be inspired, may you listen, may you trust.

Much love,

Anna

Messages of Grace

Anna Grace Taylor

1 We Exist Because You Do

We exist because you exist and are with each one of you without exception. That means all of you can also communicate with us.

Do ask us for help whenever you need it and then listen to the repetitive, loving, supportive visions, ideas, sounds or feelings you receive. These are all ways we talk to you.

Ask us for a sign today and see what you notice! We are waiting for your call.

We love you,

Your Angels

Your Thoughts

2 True Success

You are not the money you make, or the car you drive, or the number of people who know you. You are you. Stop looking outside yourself for happiness and success. When you show up in the world being true to yourself and your desires – that is success. When you touch even one person with your kindness – that is success. When you live and love as best you can – that is success. You are brilliant – right now.

We love you,

Your Angels

Your Thoughts

3 Teach by Example

There's no need to prove anything to anyone or convince them of the best way to be. There are many paths in life, and the most powerful way to teach is by example. Live and love and let everyone else travel their own journey.

We love you,

Your Angels

Your Thoughts

4 Your Sexuality

Embrace your sensuality and sexuality, dear one. It is indeed a beautiful part of your human experience. Rather than something to be ashamed of, it is truly Divine to express yourself in these ways. You are a gorgeous, attractive being and deserve to experience love, joy and pleasure in every way.

We love you,

Your Angels

Your Thoughts

5 Keep it Simple

Simplify things, dear one. You needn't do so much, have so much, want so much – and especially not if it's overwhelming you.

Life is indeed far more comfortable than you make it at times. Focus on your priorities and let go of what is not important to you so that you can create space to breathe, to live, to be.

We love you,

Your Angels

Your Thoughts

6 Don't Give Up

Don't give up before your miracle happens. We're continually working behind the scenes for you once you ask and then your job is to have faith that it is all working out in your favour. Because it always is. Even if you don't know how, or if the outcome looks slightly different from what you expected.

When you ask, remember to say, 'this or something better' so that you stay open to the best for yourself. We see the bigger picture of your life and are likely bringing you something more wonderful than you can imagine!

We love you,

Your Angels

Your Thoughts

7 Your Education

Taking a class or furthering your education can be an excellent idea. If you truly feel guided to do so, if it excites you, if it adds to your life or career, then go for it! But do not use study as an excuse to procrastinate what you know you are meant to do.

As a human being, there is always more to learn because life is a continual process, so you needn't be perfect in order to teach or share what you know, and the chances are you are ready now! Be honest with yourself about which applies to you.

We love you,

Your Angels

Your Thoughts

8 In Conflict

If you find yourself in conflict with another, remember that you cannot change anyone. If someone disagrees with you, let them. You can speak your truth and work towards a peaceful resolution if that feels appropriate.

But everyone is entitled to their beliefs, and the only person you ever have any control over is you. Seek not to control anyone but to live and let live. You are all unique threads in the same tapestry. So accept your differences of opinion whenever possible and just be true to yourself.

We love you,

Your Angels

Your Thoughts

9 Trust, Trust, Trust

What could you do if you really trusted
that you were fully supported and taken
care of at all times? What could you do
if you trusted in the Divine order of life?
Can you trust in this and all that you
are ... even just a little more today?

We love you,

Your Angels

Your Thoughts

10 What's Inspiring You?

Pay attention to your new, creative ideas! This is a fantastic time to begin working on new projects or expressing yourself in new ways. Don't worry about what others are doing or whether it's been done before. Because it's never been done by you, in your particular way.

Go with the flow of your beautiful heart. Whatever excites you, whatever moves you and inspires you is exactly what the world needs from you.

We love you,

Your Angels

Your Thoughts

About Angels

Every moment we are alive,
An Angel is always with us.
Every time we ask for help,
An Angel fulfils their purpose.
Every time we feel alone,
An Angel whispers, 'I am here'.
Every time we pray for peace,
We rest in an Angel's wings.
Every time we say yes to our joy,
An Angel rejoices.
Every time we follow our guidance,
An Angel leads the way.
Every time we have the courage to fly,
An Angel flies beside us.
Every time we live our truth,
An Angel honours us.
Every moment, no matter what,
An Angel loves us unconditionally.
And every time we open our hearts,
To say, 'I love you' and mean it,
When we support another;
When we offer hope;
When we choose to be kind,
We become Angels ourselves.

Anna Grace Taylor

11 Your Life

Your mind is fighting to give your life meaning. It's already full of meaning. Your mind is always comparing, judging and pushing to be somewhere you have yet to go. You are already here.

You are so busy trying to do, do, do, that you cannot receive the love that is given to you. Just for a moment, let love in. Allow yourself to be where you are. Be kind to yourself, and the ways you have travelled, the ways you have overcome. Stop trying to change yourself and start being kinder to yourself. That will change everything by default.

Your life is not an accident. Your place on this planet was made for you. You spend hours and days pondering the meaning of your existence, and yet every second you're breathing is full of purpose. Full of purpose because you are meant to be here. Here in this moment, just as you are.

You are not a mistake. You are not an exception to the rule. You turn yourself dizzy trying to find the answers to questions made of lies.

Because the truth is, there's only one answer. And that answer, however simple it may seem, is love.

You are love and forever loved. You might forget it. You might try to prove your worth. You might fall on your knees trying to please others who have forgotten, too. But still, you are perfect even as you sleep. Even when you can't see beyond the brokenness they've sold you. You never will be anything but beautiful to us.

We love you,

Your Angels

Your Thoughts

12 Celebrate Yourself

Celebrate your uniqueness! You are who you are for many beautiful reasons. Do not try to be someone else to please others. You don't need anyone's approval to live your life the way you want to live it. You don't need permission to do what feels good to you. But if you want it, here it is.

We love you,

Your Angels

Your Thoughts

13 True Love

We absolutely want the best for you. We truly wish you deep, true love in all of your relationships, which is why we remind you to include yourself in that love. If you are looking for another to make you happy, to complete you, or to distract you from your problems, then think again. No person can do or be that for you, even if you think they can. Come together with another knowing that they are a beautiful reflection of all the love that you are and you shall both rejoice!

We love you,

Your Angels

Your Thoughts

14 The Gift of Meditation

Spend some time in meditation today. You don't have to be in silence – even singing, dancing or washing the dishes can be a form of meditation. But just allow your mind to quieten so you can listen to our guidance. We are always with you and always answering your prayers but being quiet gives you the space to ask and to listen deeply.

We love you,

Your Angels

Your Thoughts

15 Your Inner Child

Connect with your inner child and ask how they are feeling. Listen to what they want to say and do right now. Close your eyes and spend some time checking in with your younger self and see what is revealed to you. They may want to play or cry or simply be heard. Whatever they may need, give them some love and attention. Give them space to be and let them know they matter. Because you matter. Every part of you matters and is included.

We love you,

Your Angels

Your Thoughts

16 Divine Timing

Patience, dear one. Patience. There is a Divine timing to every experience. Often, many pieces of the puzzle need to fit together before your desires can manifest. Sometimes, they may not occur as you'd hope, but as long as you ask us, we promise we're working with you behind the scenes and will always have your best interests at heart. You'll see.

We love you,

Your Angels

Your Thoughts

17 Be Kind

Carrying out a random act of kindness, for no reason other than because you want to help someone, is a beautiful way to change the world. Kindness costs nothing and can mean everything. Not just to one person but to many because of the ripple effect it can create.

Be kind. Be someone's Earth Angel!

We love you,

Your Angels

Your Thoughts

18 There is Always Hope

Never give up on yourself. There is always hope for a brighter tomorrow. And anything good can happen at any moment. Reach out for help if you need it from your loved ones, those you trust, and us, Your Angels who will believe in you until you can believe in yourself. You are never alone!

We love you,

Your Angels

Your Thoughts

19 Your Purpose

You do not need to strive to find your purpose. Your purpose is love. Your mission is to be here as you. Just follow what brings you joy, one step at a time. Follow what you are curious about. Be authentic. Share what you are guided to share. Do it with love. The rest will become clear from day to day and may change as you change. Remember, most of all that what you do is not your purpose. You already are your purpose.

We love you,

Your Angels

Your Thoughts

20 No Regrets

Do not waste your time lingering in regret. You cannot change the past, you can only choose now. If you are grateful for your life in any way then embrace every choice you ever made because each one led you here so even your seeming mistakes are Divine.

Keep the lessons and the love and let go of all the 'coulds', 'shoulds' and 'what ifs' that weigh heavy on your heart. Let yourself off the hook and let this day be one when you choose to move forward and begin again.

We love you,

Your Angels

Your Thoughts

21 Stop Comparing Yourself

We understand how tempting it is to compare yourself to others. We know how easy it is for you to judge your body, your mind, your success, your challenges, your entire life – against someone you may or may not know. But you will never truly understand what it's like to live someone else's life, so do not wish for it. Be inspired by another, learn from them, but do not try to be them. To do so is to deny the life that has been made especially for you. Don't hide the gift you are to the world. Believe in yourself. Focus on you. The you that is always, always enough.

We love you,

Your Angels

Your Thoughts

22 Boundaries

We see many of you as sensitive, loving people feeling perplexed about what it means to have healthy boundaries. Even the word boundaries can feel limiting in nature. In Divine truth, of course, we are all One, the same Source, the same love, the same expansive, infinite energy. You are me, and I am you, there is no separation.

You carry this knowledge with you, along with a great desire to be of service. You want to make a difference in a world where you all have your own bodies, your own choices and your own energy to take care of.

But as time goes on in your human experience, you start to believe, mistakenly, that to be a kind, giving person you must sacrifice your own needs and desires. You make yourself available at the expense of your own well-being. And what good does that do?

So when we speak of boundaries, we are not asking you to forget others, we are merely reminding you to take care of you. Don't dismiss your interconnectedness, but honour your individual journey upon earth. Remember that your time and energy are precious, so you get to choose how you use them.

And so for clarity, from our perspective, we offer you the following guidance:

Having boundaries does not mean isolating yourself from other people. Nor does it mean building walls, closing your heart or being rude, dismissive or uncaring. It does not mean seeing yourself as more important than others, and it certainly does not mean being selfish.

Be honest with your yes and your no. Remember that you teach people how to treat you by deciding what you will and will not accept. Similarly, maintaining boundaries means not offering unsolicited advice in an attempt to be helpful and stepping back when someone doesn't want or need your assistance.

Having compassionate boundaries means respecting others' space and your own and being mindful of your energy. It means listening to your feelings and what is important to you. When you stop giving with a sense of obligation, resentment and exhaustion, you have so much to gain: clarity, vitality and a willingness to give where and when you can.

Having boundaries means understanding that you are the only one truly responsible for your energy. Ultimately, it means taking care of yourself at the deepest level at every level. When you do, everyone benefits, beautiful one.

We love you,

Your Angels

Your Thoughts

23 Mercy

You are perfect as you are.
Human? Yes. Always remembering
love? Maybe not.

But we adore you in all your moments.
We see the best in you in all ways.
Stop beating yourself up for what you
haven't done or who you could be.
Show yourself some mercy.

We love you,

Your Angels

Your Thoughts

24 Take Care of Your Energy

If you are feeling tired, drained or unclear right now (or any time), be sure to ask Archangel Michael and all of us to clear your energy. Exhale. Give all your worries and cares to us. Imagine all the energy you're carrying that doesn't belong to you is being lifted away from you. Then imagine or feel yourself being filled with white, healing light. You may wish to take a sea-salt bath or shower. It's a fantastic way to clear and uplift your vibration. As is going out into nature or playing your favourite music.

Take care of yourself!

We love you,

Your Angels

Your Thoughts

25 You Are Beautiful

You are beautiful, just as you are. Give yourself a break and start to notice the wonderful things about yourself. Can you be kind rather than focus on all the flaws you perceive you have? Can you interrupt your critical voice for a moment and accept who you are right now? We can, and it is our greatest wish for you to see yourself as we see you.

We love you,

Your Angels

Your Thoughts

26 Make a Decision

If you have a decision to make, close your eyes and take a deep breath. Focus on making a choice (if there are multiple options, repeat this with each of them). Then breathe deep down into your heart and your stomach. Notice how making this decision feels. Do your heart and gut feel comfortable, warm, supported? Or does something feel 'off', tight, cold? Listen to your body. This is your intuition. This is how we guide you. Trust it. And if you're still not sure, come back to it later. Or perhaps consider that neither option is right for now. You'll know when it is.

We love you,

Your Angels

Your Thoughts

27 Have Fun

Have fun! Joy is your natural Divine state. When you play or do anything that lifts your heart, you automatically raise your vibration, gain clarity, and everything flows more smoothly. For that reason, fun, play and laughter are essential to your well-being and should never be underestimated.

We love you,

Your Angels

Your Thoughts

28 Look How Far You've Come

Take a moment to reflect on your journey and see how far you've come: all the ways you've learned and grown, all the obstacles you've overcome.

Your mind may often remind you of all things you have or haven't done, but just for a while, give yourself some credit for who you are and be proud! Your life is precious, and that is worth celebrating.

We love you,

Your Angels

Your Thoughts

29 Focus on What You Can Do

Life happens. Things change and feel out of your control, and we understand that this can be hard. The truth is, as much as you try, you cannot control the mystery that is your life and The Universe. But when you focus on what you can do, you'll feel empowered rather than helpless, dear one. Focus on all the blessings in your life and be grateful that you have many choices available to you even in circumstances that you didn't choose.

We love you,

Your Angels

Your Thoughts

30 The Full Moon

On the Full Moon, we encourage you to let go, let go, let go. That doesn't always need to be people or things. It can be patterns or habits you find yourself stuck in or memories from the past that hold you back. Journal. Create a ceremony. Cry. Whatever you do, honour those times. Honour your emotions. Honour your energy with each cycle as it comes and know that with every release, you can look forward to new blessings.

We love you,

Your Angels

Your Thoughts

31 Be Yourself

No one knows your truth like you do.
No one knows precisely what it's like to
be you. So stay on your own path.
Listen to your own heart. There will
always be people who do not understand
it or try to make you wrong for your
choices because they believe their way is
the right way. But you are all on earth
for different reasons, and sometimes
that means standing out and up and
saying yes to your own lives even if
others think you are crazy. You can't be
happy if you follow someone else's version
of you. So be you, just as you are.

We love you,

Your Angels

Your Thoughts

32 Your Vulnerability

Your vulnerability, as you call it, may feel profoundly exposing and scary. We honour your fear as we do every part of your experience but being honest about your feelings is a must. Your truth, however uncomfortable it seems, will indeed set you free, and there is no greater gift. We Angels love you unconditionally and rejoice in the moments when you allow others to see who you are – tears and all. For there is nothing that could match the beauty and perfection of a raw, truthful heart as it opens up to more love.

We love you,

Your Angels

Your Thoughts

An Angel Blessing

Angels around you.

Angels above you.

Angels comfort you.

Angels watch over you.

Angels beside you.

Angels within you.

Angels never judge you.

Angels always love you.

Anna Grace Taylor

33 Speak Your Truth

Speak your truth with love. Express your heart. Your passionate, honest, authentic voice is so needed in the world. Truth is so needed in the world.

However, that does not mean that it will be everyone's truth. You are not for everyone. There will be many who disagree with your message and your point of view, perhaps even your own family. We do not suggest that it is always easy, but some will want to make you wrong if you are truthful with your soul. Can you recall a single person in history that has ever been accepted and embraced by all? No. But no doubt they were powerful because they stayed in their own integrity.

Remember, do not concern yourself with those who cannot hear you, or do not understand you. We encourage you to share so that the people who resonate with you, those who can be comforted and uplifted and changed by you, can benefit from the words and the gifts that you have to offer.

Your fear may tell you that everything has already been said. That your voice is just one of millions in a sea of noise. Or even that you need to keep quiet to keep the peace. That what you have to say does not matter. But your truth is your peace and your truth does matter because you matter.

We are with you. Ask us to speak with you and through you. And then speak up because you have a voice. Speak up because you cannot stay silent any longer. Speak up for your own well-being. Speak up for your dreams. Speak up for the one who has prayed for guidance. Speak up for the one who is waiting to hear your words. Speak up and be a light in the darkness. Speak up in the name of love. Your voice is an instrument in the orchestra of The Universe. Use it, beautiful one.

We love you,

Your Angels

Your Thoughts

34 You Are So Loved

You are so, so loved and loveable. Just as you are right now. There is nothing you could say or do that changes that. You are worthy simply because you're alive. If you could see yourself as we see you, you would never doubt your beauty or your worthiness again. Ask us to help you feel and know this truth even just for a moment.

We love you,

Your Angels

Your Thoughts

35 What's Working?

Take inventory of your life. Spend some time reviewing and re-evaluating what is or isn't working for you. Declutter your space and your energy. Take time to tie up loose ends. As you take time to look within, heal and gain clarity, you create some much-needed space ready for new blessings. All is in Divine order, and you are taken care of now and always.

We love you,

Your Angels

Your Thoughts

36 We've Got You

Whenever you call, we listen.
Whenever you ask, we hear you.
Whenever you need us, we are there.

Please know you are never, ever alone
even though it may feel that way
sometimes. Breathe and relax.

Whatever is happening in your world,
we are with you. We have never left
you and never will. Rest and feel our
loving energy wrapped around you.
We've got you.

We love you,

Your Angels

Your Thoughts

37 Keep Your Heart Open

You never quite know when you will meet someone who will change your life in beautiful ways.

So keep your heart open and live your life as happily, healthily and lovingly as you can, without worrying if you are too much or too little or too weird. The right people will love you and appreciate you as you are.

We love you,

Your Angels

Your Thoughts

38 Count Your Blessings

Count your blessings, dear one.
However small they may seem.
Let gratitude lift you up and out of
victimhood and into empowerment.

Focus upon what is good in your life,
and we promise that more reasons to be
grateful shall come to you. Not because
you are more deserving – you're always
deserving. But because your energy
becomes wide open to the blessings that
have been and always will be yours.

Forever and ever.

We love you,

Your Angels

Your Thoughts

39 If You Are Feeling Anxious

If you are feeling anxious, we invite you to focus on your breath and come back here. Here in this moment where all is well.

Don't fuel your anxiety by racing ahead into the future and worrying about what might happen. Nor by re-living something that has already happened. It is indeed your powerful imagination working over-time trying desperately to be in control.

We invite you to ponder the fact that you cannot control The Universe or anyone in it. You never could. All you can do is make choices that support your well-being, reach out for help when you need it, and whenever you can, bring yourself back to now, the only time that's guaranteed.

We love you,

Your Angels

Your Thoughts

40 Money, Money, Money

You are connected to an infinite stream of abundance and live on a plentiful earth. Open your arms and your heart to receive all its gifts, including money! It is merely the current of energy you use as a physical exchange in your human experience and needn't be seen or experienced with such judgement.

All of your needs are taken care of, now and always. Believe it. Allow it. And know that when you do, you are far more able to live and be of service in the ways you wish.

We love you,

Your Angels

Your Thoughts

41 Love Goes On

Is your heart healing from a relationship ending? Perhaps you're grieving the loss of a loved one in heaven? Or you are questioning what on earth is going on? Just remember that love is never-ending.

You are love – and that love lives forever! Nothing is ever lost, no-one is ever gone. Love connects us all, and the rest are details in this experience you call life. Nevertheless, we comfort you now and any time you ask.

We love you,

Your Angels

Your Thoughts

42 Your Real Power

Power is not about force, aggression or control; neither is it measured by status or career. Those are all fear-based perspectives that focus on your differences.

Your real power is love, where you are all equally worthy, special and capable with your own beautiful lessons and experiences. Use your power to make a difference in the world.

We love you,

Your Angels

Your Thoughts

43 Delays and Detours

Do not let some bumps in the road stop you from achieving what you want to, or going where you want to go. Sometimes the delays or changes to plans are so that you take a different route or to make you take a temporary pause.

That said, if something continually feels wrong about the path you are taking, consider it a sign to re-evaluate your desires. Sometimes what you think you want might not be for your highest good. Either way, keep believing in your dreams and be open to the way they come to you!

We love you,

Your Angels

Your Thoughts

An Angel Prayer

Thank you, Angels, for being here with me.
For surrounding me with your love.
For reminding me that I AM love.

Thank you for helping me trust that I am
forever connected to you.
For giving me guidance I can easily understand.
For giving me the courage to follow it,
one step at a time.

Thank you for supporting me as I shine my light.
For leading me to beautiful opportunities.
For helping me embrace my gifts
and learn from my challenges.

Thank you for uplifting my mind
and opening my heart.
For all the blessings and miracles in my life.
For reminding me that I AM a miracle.

Anna Grace Taylor

44 Your Light

There is a light within you. A light that is you. Like the Sun, it is always there even when it seems hidden by the clouds. A light that says, 'I'll try again tomorrow'. A light that makes everything clearer and brighter. This light is entirely inextinguishable and infinite. The light of a million stars. The light of a hundred thousand Angels.

Your light is not separate from us. You are an extension of the Divine that you call upon. When you call upon the light, you are indeed asking for a reminder of you. The you that is connected to All That Is. You are calling upon you, the magnificent you that has been brought to earth to share your light in human form; the you that is powerful beyond measure.

Do not be afraid of your light. Shine it brightly. You were born to shine! For your light can do no harm, and those who feel threatened or intimidated by your light are simply afraid of their own. Do not let them deter you but equally do not force your light upon others.

Your light is indeed a powerful force in the world but it need not be forced.

Your light is your light. Just be the light. Let it go where it goes. Shine because it makes you feel good, shine for all the people who are ready to wake up from their slumber, shine for all the hearts who are meant to find you.

Do not be fooled, however, into thinking that your light must be drained to help another. Be a beacon, be a lighthouse, be a guide for those who should find themselves struggling. But remember that you are not their source of light. Your light is your light. Their light is theirs. By owning your light by standing in your truth, you light the way for others to come back to theirs and one by one, light shines around the world. Your light is so needed. Keep showing up. Keep shining. Thank you, beautiful one.

We love you,

Your Angels

Your Thoughts

45 Mother Nature

If you need a new perspective or inspiration, we encourage you to get outside in nature. It is here you will often be more able to receive our guidance clearly and feel connected to all the abundant possibilities of life.

If you could do with feeling more grounded, do not underestimate the power of hugging a tree or walking directly on the earth. Feel the energy of beautiful Mother Earth and let her support you.

We love you,

Your Angels

Your Thoughts

46 Life is Precious

Life is precious, dear one. Live it and love it the best you can because while your soul is eternal, your earthly life can change in a second and all you will take with you as you leave, is the love and joy.

You won't hold on to all the things you stress about now. So embrace the present moment and love, love, love each other!

We love you,

Your Angels

Your Thoughts

47 Romance

You deserve a beautiful love life!

Do you believe that? Are you hesitating? Then it's time to focus on who you really are – a passionate, attractive being who has come here to experience pleasure and love in every way!

Ask us to help you feel it from within and put romance 'back on the table' in your life, because honestly, it never left in the first place.

We love you,

Your Angels

Your Thoughts

48 A Big Hug

If you are feeling sad today, be kind to yourself. Take some time to be quiet, cry, write in your journal, go for a walk.

Whatever you need. It's OK to reach out for help too because you *all* have days that are challenging. In the meantime, consider yourself hugged by all of us.

We love you,

Your Angels

Your Thoughts

49 Ask and You Shall Receive

There is no limit to what you can ask us to help you with. We are limitless energy. It is only you as human beings who believe in and experience limitation. And don't forget, we love you, unconditionally, and we exist to support you in your earthly life in all ways. So you have every reason to ask and to receive.

We love you,

Your Angels

Your Thoughts

50 You Are All Equal

We encourage you not to focus on your differences but on the ways that you are all Divine beings having a human experience. All wanting peace, all learning to give and receive love, all doing the best you can.

Your ego may have you believe you are less than or better than another, but you are all equal in the eyes of God, and therefore there is no need to compare yourself.

You are all loved without exception.

We love you,

Your Angels

Your Thoughts

51 The Power of Your Words

Your words hold immense power. Choose lovingly and kindly so that you can contribute to healing, not breaking, hearts.

You are not responsible for the feelings of others, but you can do your best to treat others how you'd want to be treated and then love goes on and on.

We love you,

Your Angels

Your Thoughts

52 Dream Big

Are you dreaming BIG enough? Do you still believe in your heart's real desires, or have you let the fear or the well-meaning opinions of others stop you from pursuing your dreams?

Today, we encourage you to re-commit yourself to your passions and that which lights you up, because dear one, that is your soul calling you. That is your answer.

Never settle for less than what you want just because someone else believes you can't have it. You get to decide.

We love you,

Your Angels

Your Thoughts

53 Time Out

You don't need permission to rest and be quiet, but if you need a reminder to allow yourself to take time out, here it is. Take care of yourself; nurture your mind, body and spirit.

Know that when you do, you'll have the energy to get things done more efficiently and easily later. Breathe and give yourself some quiet time as soon as you can.

We love you,

Your Angels

Your Thoughts

54 Your People

Surround yourself with people who see the best in you, who celebrate your victories as they would their own and who comfort your tears and fears without defining you by them.

If you do not have these kinds of friendships in your life, then ask us to help you find them and believe you deserve them.

We love you,

Your Angels

Your Thoughts

55 Be With Your Pain

Be with your pain; let it breathe. Give it life. Get it out. Do not try to make yourself OK for fear of falling apart. Perhaps you might, but the truth of you remains. The only things that may fall away are the past, the lies, the trap of comparison, the snare of the mind that is desperately trying to control every little thing.

We have much compassion for the mind; it has brought you far in ways necessary for your human experience. We understand that you often feel confined by limitation, by what you have learned; by what others see as reality. We encourage you not to judge your current pain but to allow it to move through you. To make it a reason to call upon support and to listen to your heart. To let your lack of faith at this moment, be the moment you drop deeper into your heart, into the place that is not of understanding but of being.

So, this heartbreak you feel is indeed a breaking open of your heart and the falling apart you are so afraid of is indeed part of your awakening.

For when there is nothing on earth that makes sense, when you are down to your last drop of faith, your true heart speaks. Your truth emerges.

The depth of your desire rises up, above your fear and you welcome the miracles into your life that have always been here for you – that are you.

It isn't that you must suffer if you want to grow, heal or experience miracles. Still, we see that in your efforts to be OK with how your life has been – in your choice to remain comfortable in what feels less than magical to you – you do not see what is truly possible. When there seems nothing left but for a miracle to be shown to you; when it feels as if this is your only option before you break, more profound clarity and truth emerges.

Please know you are safe and we've got you. Be in this moment. Rest in the love, which is everlasting and unending regardless of your tears, your fears and your struggles. The struggle will lessen if you remember that you needn't figure anything out now. The fight to do so will only keep you stuck in your mind, which rarely has any sustaining answers and is never the seed from which miracles are born.

You are about to go deeper. You are about to live fuller. You are about to love more than you have ever known. But for now, be in the grief for what has or has not happened. Let the voice of fear have full range if that is what it needs. Just remember that you are loved more than you know. We hold you through it all and see that your light shines even brighter than before, beautiful one.

We love you,

Your Angels

Your Thoughts

56 Own Your Magnificence

Self-confidence is not about ego; it is about honouring you. It is about remembering that you are indeed a Divine being who is entirely loved and loveable. It is sharing who you are unapologetically and owning your gifts. It is caring about others without letting their opinions define you.

Though, as you stand in your truth and have confidence in yourself, others will very often have faith in you. Own your magnificence.

We love you,

Your Angels

Your Thoughts

57 Turn Your Worries into Prayers

If you are struggling right now, turn your worries into prayers for help. Sometimes we see you focusing solely on the problem rather than allowing us (or other people) to help you.

Shift your focus to what you truly desire right now and allow yourself to be supported. Miracles happen when you do!

We love you,

Your Angels

Your Thoughts

58 The New Moon

On the New Moon, we remind you to focus your energy on what you wish to invite into your life.

We understand that it's easy to go into fear about what is or isn't happening. However, rather than use your precious energy going over and over the pain and lack, let us support you to be clear about what you do want. Then we can help you co-create the life of your dreams.

Feel your desires as if they are already here because, in truth, they are! Believe and then let us help you.

We love you,

Your Angels

Your Thoughts

59 Who You Were Born to Be

Staying in your truth and integrity may not always be the easiest thing to do. In fact, it will often feel hard. But it can be hard and also feel right – deep down in your bones.

There will be times when you must be willing to disappoint another to be true to your own heart, and that's OK. Because your peace, your well-being, your best life depends on it.

Be who you are, dance to the beat of your own drum. You were born to be you, and that is more than enough – that is perfect!

We love you,

Your Angels

Your Thoughts

60 The Source of Your Happiness

You are indeed a powerful Divine being with the ability to create your own experience.

Do not give your power away to others by seeing them as the source of your happiness or unhappiness, abundance or lack. Instead, choose your own reactions, make your own decisions and live the life *you* desire! There is only one you.

We love you,

Your Angels

Your Thoughts

61 The Art of Attraction

You are all beautiful and attractive in your own way. We understand that many of you do not believe that your attractiveness has everything to do with your energy, but it's true. Otherwise everyone would be drawn to the same few.

Let your uniqueness be your sexiness. Let your heart be your sexiness. Feel it from within. Appreciate all that you are and those who genuinely appreciate you will be drawn to you like a magnet. You are magic.

We love you,

Your Angels

Your Thoughts

62 Your Guilt and Shame

Your guilt and shame may feel valid to you, but all they do is hold you hostage and cause you deep pain. They do not serve you or anyone. They only keep you trapped in the past; in the horrible lie that you are wrong, somehow flawed and unlovable.

Your human life is full of ups and downs indeed but nothing you could ever do or not do, be or not be, makes you any less loved or worthy. Drop the knife that you have held at your throat. It's time.

We love you,

Your Angels

Your Thoughts

63 The Love You Give

Keep your heart open to love, and your eyes open to the truth. Meaning, you can love everyone, but sometimes to be kind to yourself, you must love them from a distance. Being loving does not mean being a doormat. Being loving does not mean you have to put up with less than you deserve. Being loving means including yourself in the love you so freely give.

We love you,

Your Angels

Your Thoughts

64 Enjoy the Journey

Do not allow the details of life to drag you down too much. Instead, focus on what truly matters. No matter what is going on, there is always something to be grateful for, and you needn't have everything figured out to be at peace. In fact, you will never have everything figured out, so just enjoy the journey as much as you can.

We love you,

Your Angels

Your Thoughts

65 Manifestation

Let go of the 'how' and focus upon your desire. Let go of the 'when' and focus upon being ready now. Fill yourself up with the feeling of joy and excitement of your dreams being already here. Then there shall be no gap between where you are and what you want. And, dear one, let go of any fear about actually having all you have ever dreamed of. It is not only possible, but it's real.

You deserve every blessing in the world. Yes, you do.

We love you,

Your Angels

Your Thoughts

66 Your Body

Imagine a faithful friend who has walked this earth with you since you were born. A constant companion, carrying you through every moment; supporting you in many ways through every celebration and challenge. This friend is your body. The body you chose for this lifetime. Your body full of millions of cells all working together to keep you alive. You are a living, breathing miracle.

And yet, we see you treat this miraculous friend like it is your greatest enemy – with relentless comparison, disapproval, shame and downright hatred. We have deep compassion for your suffering and realise that staying in your body, let alone appreciating it can often feel like the hardest thing to do. But your dissatisfaction creates more disharmony and dis-ease, perpetuating a cycle of self-criticism.

Also, we see that you many of you have been led to believe that to live a 'spiritual' life and to feel more connected to us, you must somehow transcend your physicality.

You are indeed so much more than your body. Still, the paradox is that as you begin to own it, to move and stretch and play to root yourself to the earth, you will become aware that your body is indeed your anchor.

It allows you to easily recognise the flow of love and guidance we share with you. For you are a Divine being having a human experience and every part of you is sacred.

So, instead of being quick to notice your flaws, lumps and bumps, the pain, the things that aren't quite working as you wish they would, we ask that you stop for a moment and listen.

Listen to your body. It's likely speaking to you. How does it feel right now? What does it need? Is it asking for nourishment, for rest, or perhaps most of all, a shift in perspective?

Isn't it amazing how far you have travelled together and how much you've overcome? Isn't it amazing what it's done for you even in the midst of your suffering? Isn't it amazing how it's teaching you all the time?

It has, no matter what your circumstances, been given to you as a great gift. It is the reason you get to be here on this planet.

So honour your body as if it were a holy vessel. Because it is. Treat your body as if it were your closest confidant. Because it is. Listen to your body as if it were your guide. Because it is. Enjoy your body as if it were given to you to experience exquisite pleasure. Because it is.

Inhale these words. Let them be your prayer. Let them seep into your skin and settle in your bones.

Catch a glimpse of yourself in the mirror and give yourself the chance to see your body as we do.

Your appearance does not define you by any means. But you are not beautiful in spite of your body, you are beautiful, including your body. Embrace it, beautiful one.

We love you,

Your Angels

Your Thoughts

67 Age is Just a Number

Do not let your years on the planet tell you what you should or should not be doing. Do not wait because you are 'young' or give up because you are 'old'. Time does not reflect the depth of your beauty, courage or wisdom, because it does not define who you are. Nor should it limit your capabilities or your opportunities to form wonderful, fulfilling relationships.

Some of the most profound words you've ever heard have been spoken by a child, and many of your friends were born decades before you. A connection is a connection. Love is love. Life is life. Live it now.

We love you,

Your Angels

Your Thoughts

68 You Are Safe

You are safe, breathe out fear.

You are safe, breathe in love.

Breathe out doubt. Breathe in trust.

You are safe, and we are with you.

Call on us right now to help you, and do so any time you need.

We love you,

Your Angels

Your Thoughts

69 Take Action

Your hopes and dreams are within reach. If you can dream it, you can have it. But rather than just make a wish and then wait for it to arrive at your doorstep, we encourage you to take action when we guide you through your inspired thoughts, feelings and visions. Indeed, instant manifestations do occur.

But we often lead you to your desires and see you are looking in the other direction or simply not listening, dear one. Take that step. Take that step that you know you need to take and then we'll share another with you. You are guided and supported always!

We love you,

Your Angels

Your Thoughts

70 Like Attracts Like

'Be the change'. You hear that so much, we know. But it's just a reminder that if you want more peace in your relationships, nurture your own peace. If you yearn to feel more loved, look in the mirror and be kind to you. If you want more fun, make room for fun. If you want more abundance, notice the abundance already in your life and be grateful.

You must be what you desire because like attracts like. Energy meets energy.

We love you,

Your Angels

Your Thoughts

71 Love Does Not Hurt

Love is Love. It does not hurt. Your circumstances, the choices you or another make may cause pain, but love itself doesn't hurt.

If you are doubtful about your relationship or are being hurt in any way, love yourself enough to let go, or get support to make healthy changes. If someone is really meant for you, it'll be obvious.

We repeat: Love does not hurt.

We love you,

Your Angels

Your Thoughts

72 You Matter

Your happiness and contentment matter. You matter. You do. You do. You do. It isn't selfish to focus on the things that light you up. You do not become a better person, parent, friend for continually sacrificing your own fulfilment for another. You become drained and resentful. When you follow what feels right to you, you inspire countless others to do so, too.

So with that in mind, what choices can you make today that bring you joy or lead you towards it?

We love you,

Your Angels

Your Thoughts

73 Life is a Miracle

Miracles occur all the time. They are happening right now because life is a miracle if you choose to see it that way. You are a miracle.

Open your heart and your eyes to all the beauty within and around you. Even if it's just one thing that warms your heart or makes you smile. Then an ordinary day can become extraordinary, and everything you do has more meaning.

We love you,

Your Angels

Your Thoughts

74 Be love

Be love and allow yourself to love who you are so that you can love everyone else more wholly.

There is no search required. No pushing. No trying to be anything. Just being alive and living for love is enough. Some people may not understand or indeed even recognise that. But being love, amongst all your humanity, is what awakens the world more than anything else. Embodying it. Embracing it.

We love you,

Your Angels

Your Thoughts

75 Spread Your Wings

It is time to spread your wings and explore new things! If you want to experience something different, you may have to do something different.

If you wait until you feel fully ready for something, you may always have reason to hold yourself back and so be waiting forever. Let your heart guide you now and know that some of the best things occur when you step outside of your comfort zone.

We are here for you and urge you to ask us for whatever support you need.

We love you,

Your Angels

Your Thoughts

76 Take Nothing Personally

If someone is mean or harsh to you, please do not take it personally. Anyone happy and at peace does not need to be mean to anyone, so how they react says more about them than you.

You're responsible for your peace and your peace only. So focus on that and lead by example.

We love you,

Your Angels

Your Thoughts

77 Your Fear

Your fear will always tell you that you're not ready, incapable, unqualified and unworthy. It will have you believe that you're not good enough and that everyone else is better than you.

It will focus on all your flaws and try to fix and control you. It will give you every reason why you can't, shouldn't and won't. It will try to trip you up at every hurdle and even tell you've failed before you've even started. It will say that you don't have the money, the time, the energy. It will be full of excuses.

It will cleverly disguise itself as procrastination and perfectionism; telling you that you just need to learn a bit more, wait a bit longer. It will tell you you're too old, that you've missed your chance. Or that you're too young and you have no idea what you're talking about. It will say, 'Who do you think you are?'

Where it can often make you feel like an imposter in your own life, it can just as quickly have you believe that you are superior. It will tell you that your way is the best. It will tell you your religion is the only truth; it will tell you that you are more spiritual; it will tell you that your judgement isn't judging. It will convince you that your prejudice is reasonable. It will define others by their race, sexuality, money. It will focus on all your differences and try to separate you all in every way possible.

It will keep you from connecting, from relating, from remembering that you all belong to each other.

There will be days when it will be loud, overbearing, paralysing and may even have you believe that you exist for no reason at all; that the world is a bad place.

Fear, beautiful one, is a part of your human experience, but it does not have to rule it.

Acknowledge it, let it speak and then let it know that despite its well-meaning attempts to keep you safe, it can take a break.

Give yourself a hug. Remind yourself that everything is going to be OK even if it doesn't feel like it. Then make the conscious decision every day, to focus instead on the gentler, yet ever-powerful voice that knows there is nothing random or accidental about your existence. And that even though you will likely come face to face with fear again, and be tempted by its sneaky ways, you can, in this moment, come back to your heart, take a deep breath and say, 'I'll live anyway. I'll love anyway. I am here anyway.'

We are with you, beautiful one.

We love you,

Your Angels

Your Thoughts

78 Your Mind, Body and Spirit

As part of your self-care, we encourage you to do what you can to make healthy choices for your mind, body and spirit. Pay attention to how you spend your time, the company you keep, the things you watch, the food and drink you consume, the sleep you have. Are they supporting and uplifting you? Or are they draining you?

Be honest with yourself about any improvements that can be made to give you more energy and a sense of well-being. Every small, positive change can make a big difference.

We love you,

Your Angels

Your Thoughts

79 The Children

Pay attention to the children in your life, dear one. They may be younger than you, but their pure, open hearts are perfect teachers so do not discount their feelings or words. Listen to them. Help them feel safe to share their feelings. Let their innocence be a reminder of your own. Celebrate their individuality.

Love them, guide them, support them but let them be who they are. Let them forge their own path. And remember they do not need you to be perfect. They need you to be true to yourself so that they understand they can be, too.

We love you,

Your Angels

Your Thoughts

80 Move Forward

Have the courage to move forward. It may seem like you have to take a giant leap but any action in the direction of your most authentic desires, your heart, your dreams is enough. It may be that for the highest vision for your life to arrive, you need to move past what feels comfortable to you.

Still, please know that as you stretch yourself in this way, you are honouring your heart and saying yes to the best for you. You can do it!

We love you,

Your Angels

Your Thoughts

81 You Belong

Stop looking for somewhere to belong, someone to belong to. You belong simply because you are alive. And no-one can complete you. You are already perfect, whole and complete just as you are and so loved and loveable.

You don't need to be more deserving of love because you already are love. There is no search required. Let the love that you are lead you to the beautiful places that resonate with you, and souls with whom you can share your already blessed life.

We love you,

Your Angels

Your Thoughts

82 The Cycles of Life

If you feel in need of rest or want to take things slowly now, don't try to be busy. Similarly, make the most of your energy if you feel inspired and motivated.

There is a time for action and a time for contemplation. A time to be productive and a time to just be. Trust whatever phase you find yourself in, honour the cycles of life and know that nothing ever stays the same.

We love you,

Your Angels

Your Thoughts

83 Receive, Receive, Receive

You live on a planet with over seven billion others. You are not meant to do everything alone. As you allow yourself to receive, you have more to give to others and the beautiful cycle of giving and receiving continues.

Remember how good it feels to lift someone up? Do not deny another that feeling. And as for us, we are always here to support you without condition or limitation.

We love you,

Your Angels

Your Thoughts

84 You Are Not Broken

You are not broken. There is nothing to fix. You are not wrong. You are not a mistake. Despite your human challenges, illnesses and pains, for which we have great compassion and respect, you *are* Divinely perfect, whole and complete right now. We hold this space for you always.

No matter what. You are a miracle. Thank you for being the bright, beautiful soul that you are.

We love you,

Your Angels

Your Thoughts

85 Changes

Do not be afraid of change, dear one. Change is constant, which means uncertainty is, too. Embrace the ebb and flow, the twists and turns, the delays and the sudden momentum. Expect the unexpected. Stay open to the mystery.

Often, the changes that make no sense at the time are answers to your prayers. You are ever-changing, ever-growing, ever-moving on your beautiful journey. And we are ever-present. Wherever you are, so are we.

We love you,

Your Angels

Your Thoughts

86 Your Parents

Whatever relationship you have had or not had with your parents, know that like everyone, they did the best they could with what they knew at the time. Take time to reflect and be grateful for the role they played in giving you life, and for all the lessons you have learned from each other.

Remember too, especially if you had a complicated relationship, that your family goes way beyond those who raised you. Many beautiful souls are destined to meet, love and nurture you throughout the stages of your life. Open your heart. More of them are about to connect with you.

We love you,

Your Angels

Your Thoughts

87 Surrender

Surrendering does not mean giving up. It means letting go of how something may happen so that there is room for miracles to occur.

It means remembering that there is a Divine plan at work that can unfold when you stop trying to control the outcome. We've got you. Let go and let us help you.

We love you,

Your Angels

Your Thoughts

Angel Affirmations

Use these affirmations to help you invoke your Angels'
presence and to welcome their guidance and support.

I AM enough.

I AM always connected to Divine love,
guidance and wisdom.

I AM a powerful Divine being and I allow my light
to shine brightly.

I AM open to my Angels' messages. I listen. I trust.
I take guided action.

I allow myself to receive blessings
in every area of my life.

I AM open to miracles.

I AM surrounded by Angels now and always.

I choose to listen to love

I AM love.

I AM.

88 Be Present

This moment, this moment right now is yours, and now is all that truly exists. Yesterday has gone and tomorrow has not yet arrived. Stay here where all is well. For when you try to be somewhere other than where you are, it becomes exhausting. When you try to push forward or back, that is where your unease grows. Stress, anxiety and worry are felt when you try to re-live the past or figure out the future. Stay here. Breathe. Be present in this moment. It is a gift.

And the greatest gift you can give another is your presence. Your presence that says,

'I am fully here with you. You are important to me. This moment matters to me. There is nowhere I need to be right now other than here.'

Your life is full of endless choices and plans but do not be so busy chasing the next idea, the next dream, the next thing to do that you forget the beauty right in front of you. Happiness is not over there, it is already here.

Peace is not when you get somewhere, it is here. You can wait and wait and wait for another now that will be better. Yet there is no now other than this moment. You can do and do and do to get to the next thing. But it will never be now. There is no guarantee other than now.

So live it. Cherish it. Be in it. In this moment. Feel your heart beating. Feel the air in your lungs. Your chest rising and falling. Feel your feet on the ground. Centre yourself in this moment. Let whatever you feel just be. Can you allow this moment to be enough, for you to be enough right now? For where you are to be where you are and let each moment guide you to the next? Your path will unfold step by step and your future moments will be created with far more joy when you decide to be here now.

Always, beautiful one.

We love you,

Your Angels

Your Thoughts

89 Be Creative

Be more creative. Sing. Dance. Write. Paint. Whether you share what you create with the world or not, does not matter.

What matters is that you give yourself time and space to tap into the magic that flows through you and express it. When you do, you are allowing who you truly are – a beautiful, talented, creative being – to relax and shine.

We love you,

Your Angels

Your Thoughts

90 The Opportunity in Envy

When you find yourself feeling envious of another, it is an opportunity for you to recognise what you truly want. When you admire someone's life or accomplishments, it's because very similar energy, similar dreams are calling you. Very rarely are you envious of something that does not interest you. So be grateful for your moment of longing and the seeming lack of what you are not yet experiencing. Then shift your focus. Recognise that what you desire is available to you, too.

No one is more special or more deserving than you. You are all equally worthy and can experience your own joy in your own ways. Let envy be a reminder to take action to make your own dreams come true.

We love you,

Your Angels

Your Thoughts

91 Your Disappointments

Do not let past disappointments rule your decisions, wondering, 'What if that happens again?' Ask yourself what you have learned from previous experiences that can support you now and let this experience be new.

Be optimistic. Don't allow your past to squash your future. What if the best was yet to come? Isn't that worth moving forward for? You can do it, and we are with you all the way.

We love you,

Your Angels

Your Thoughts

92 The Voice of Love

We, Your Angels, are the voice of love. This voice will never make you feel bad, will never put you down. Will always encourage and support you, and see the best in you.

The guidance we give you may not always make sense, and it won't always be easy, but it will be consistent and clear and will feel right deep in your gut. Listen.

We love you,

Your Angels

Your Thoughts

93 Your Home

Do you feel at home where you are? And by that we mean, do you feel comfortable in your space? Is it time for you to clear the energy of your surroundings, make changes or even move to a new place?

If you've been getting the message to do one or all of these, then this is confirmation. Home is indeed where the heart is, but if your heart isn't enjoying your space, then it's time to listen.

We love you,

Your Angels

Your Thoughts

94 No Matter What

We have deep compassion for your struggles, and we are with you through them all. However, we see far beyond your pain, your mistakes, your worries and your fears. We hold the highest vision for you always.

The same miracles and the same mysterious, wondrous beauty that led you to this moment made you who you are. And it will continue to carry you through. No matter what happens.

We love you,

Your Angels

Your Thoughts

95 Through a Child's Eyes

See the world through a child's eyes. Look around you and see all the possibilities available to you. Let the flowers and the trees and the big blue sky remind you of the miracle of life.

Play. Laugh. Be free of responsibility for a while. Be present in this moment.
It is a gift. You are a gift.

We love you,

Your Angels

Your Thoughts

96 Soulmates

Soulmates are not always partners.
They can be friends, family, or even
people you meet for a fleeting moment.
They will teach you, often shake you,
and wake you up, and you will likely do
the same for them.

But the connection, the familiarity you
feel within your heart is undeniable.
Be thankful for those people with whom
you share your life, who beyond any
details, ultimately cross your path to
remind you of who you are.

We love you,

Your Angels

Your Thoughts

97 Every Ending

If you are experiencing an ending in your life now, we want you to know that you are not alone and that we hold you through what may be a painful time for you.

We know it is far from easy to let go, especially when it involves something or someone you love. Allow yourself to grieve, to cry, to be angry, not to understand any of it.

Be gentle with yourself as you heal. Honour what or who is leaving, but know that with every goodbye, we bring you a hello. We bring you the opportunity to begin again.

We love you,

Your Angels

Your Thoughts

98 Easy Does It

Easy does it. You cannot force anything to happen. Remember that if something is meant for you, it shall be in perfect timing. That's not to say you have to sit back and do nothing for your desire to manifest.

But having faith means trusting the journey you are on, and understanding that life is working for you and not against you. That includes rejection, which is indeed our protection, and delays which are often detours designed for your highest good. Trust. There is a Divine plan for your life, which is far greater than you can imagine.

We love you,

Your Angels

Your Thoughts

Come to the Edge: An Awakening

Come to the edge, she said.
The edge of the end.
The edge of a new beginning.
The edge of nothing and everything.
The edge of hopelessness and despair;
Where all is battered and broken to be rebuilt.
All is emptied to become full.

Come to the edge, she said.
The edge of goodbye.
The edge of the great hello.
The edge of utterly lost and found.
The edge of absolutely null and void.
The hole where all is whole and perfectly imperfect.
All is forgotten to be remembered.

Come to the edge, she said.
The edge of darkness.
The edge of the brightest light.
The edge of beauty and disaster
The edge of chaos and silence,
Where no words are enough and anything is possible.
All is breathless to be re-born.

Anna Grace Taylor

99 Forgiveness

We understand that when you may have experienced extremely challenging situations, forgiveness can often feel like the most impossible task.

But we want to remind you that forgiveness does not mean condoning human behaviour; nor does it mean that someone who has hurt you has to remain in your life. Sometimes they will, and sometimes they won't. Sometimes forgiveness happens in a moment. For many of you, though, forgiveness can be a much longer healing process. Don't feel bad about being unable to forgive, because that only gives you even more reason to feel bad. Be where you are. You needn't try to force it.

Either way, we will say this: forgiveness is for you. Forgiveness is always about you. Forgiveness is remembering that despite your mistakes, or those of another, you are, and have always been, entirely loveable.

From our perspective, you are all indeed innocent children, and nothing you could do could alter our love for you. It is truly unconditional.

With this in mind, we hope that today or someday, you will be willing to release the pain of the past that has become so heavy on your heart and move forward into more peace. Forgive yourself. Forgive those who forgot the Divine truth of who they are and perhaps caused you to forget, too. Forgive and set yourself free at the deepest level.

We love you,

Your Angels

Your Thoughts

100 The Beauty in Your Fragility

To wear your heart on your sleeve, to feel deeply, to love fiercely, is often viewed as being 'too vulnerable'. True, you must take care of your energy, but being emotional is not a weakness. Neither is asking for help. So do reach out if you need to.

Call upon us, and your fellow human beings for support. There is beauty in the most fragile of moments. Embrace it all, as we embrace you.

We love you,

Your Angels

Your Thoughts

101 Your Breath

The power of your breath is amazing. Use it consciously to let go, to energise, to relax, to find your centre, to connect to us. Take a moment to breathe deeply and evenly. In and out like the tide.

Breathe in, as if you are inhaling the scent of a beautiful rose, whatever you may need. Breathe out, as if you are blowing out a candle, and give all your tension to us. Just breathe and be. Ahh, that feels good, doesn't it?

We love you,

Your Angels

Your Thoughts

102 Self-Love

Self-love is not about holding yourself to extremely high standards. It isn't about giving yourself a list of things to aspire to be or practise so that you can feel good or be loved by another. That isn't very loving at all, is it? We encourage you, instead, to be self-kind.

Take good care of your precious body, honour your needs and desires, speak to yourself as you would a friend. And most of all, remember that you don't need to be perfect as a human being, because as a Divine being you already are.

We love you,

Your Angels

Your Thoughts

103 One Step at a Time

If something feels overwhelming, too big or too far away, just take one step towards it. You needn't do everything at once, but as you ask for our assistance, each level will be revealed to you.

While instant miracles can and do happen, often the miracles you experience occur because you've taken action in your physical world. So ask, listen, take guided action, have faith and know that we are supporting you always. You are not meant to do anything alone. We are your greatest supporters and cheerleaders.

We love you,

Your Angels

Your Thoughts

104 You Are All Spiritual

No one is superior to anyone else. No person is more, or less, spiritual because you are all spiritual beings having a human experience. It's simply that some are more aware of this truth and live it more consciously.

If someone acts as if they have everything figured out or tries to make you feel less than you are, trust that it's simply a cover-up for their own pain. Stay centred in your experience and know that you are always connected to Divine love and wisdom. You are Divine love and wisdom.

We love you,

Your Angels

Your Thoughts

105 Feel What You Feel

It is safe for you to feel your feelings. Let them move through you like a river. You will not drown, no matter how intense they may be. Despite what you may have been taught, no emotions are wrong – it is when you try to suppress or hide them, that they become heavier and have more power over you.

Your feelings are simply asking you to listen to what is going on within and around you. As you give them space, it'll become much easier to find relief and peace. We're with you.

We love you,

Your Angels

Your Thoughts

106 Music is Your Friend

Music is often known as your universal language because its ability to unite you all is unparalleled. Do not underestimate its powerful impact on you. There is a reason we often speak to you through music and why it moves so many of you like nothing else. As a vibrational being, any sound you listen to can literally shift your energy.

Enjoy it. Play it. Dance to it. Sing with it. Let it soothe you and free you and uplift you. Let it be your friend. You are indeed an instrument in the orchestra of life.

We love you,

Your Angels

Your Thoughts

107 You Are Enough

Do not let the need for perfection keep you stuck in procrastination. Don't wait around for everything to be 'just right' before you do anything; otherwise, you will wait forever.

Instead, we encourage you to begin; continue, create and learn as you go along. Share what you can from where you are as that is always enough.

You are enough.

We love you

Your Angels

Your Thoughts

108 The Fire Inside You

There's a fire inside of you. A passionate fire that is always burning but often buried by responsibilities, the need to please others, or the belief that your own desires are selfish.

You might feel OK. But what if there is more? Make a decision to reconnect to the fire deep within you. Let it burn away the old and set your heart alight. This is life.

We love you,

Your Angels

Your Thoughts

109 While You Are Sleeping

Pay attention to your dreams now because they are offering you insights. When your body is asleep, and your conscious mind is resting, and out of the way, we can share guidance with you more easily. Your soul is also free to travel.

So if you wake with a feeling that you've been somewhere or with someone, trust that. We are all connected, and life is so much more than you can comprehend.

We love you,

Your Angels

Your Thoughts

110 The Answers You Seek

By all means, seek comfort, reassurance, guidance and support from your fellow human beings. That is all part of sharing and growing and learning together.

But do not rely on another's wisdom. You know what to do. All the answers you seek are within you. Trust yourself and trust that we are guiding you always.

We love you,

Your Angels

Your Thoughts

111 Your Sensitivity

You may be told you're too sensitive, too much, too weird. You may often feel like you've been dropped off on planet earth and that few understand you. So, sweet one, we want you to know that we understand you, we see you. We see the strength and the courage it has taken you to get here, to walk through a world that can feel so heavy and hold on to hope in the darkest of times.

We see it all, your beauty and how much you give to others without the thought of recognition or reward. We know the way you change lives just by being you.

Thank you. Thank you for never giving up because the world needs the magic only you can share, and the things that have made you feel so different are the very reasons you are alive at this time.

Never let your sensitivity stop you. Let it become your superpower.

Never let your sensitivity stress you. Let it be felt as the strength within you.

Never let your sensitivity silence you. Let it be heard in your song and your story. Never let your sensitivity scare you. Let it be known as your sacred gift.

Never let your sensitivity separate you. Let it be felt as the sexiest thing about you. Never let your sensitivity shrink you. Let it be a reason to shine in all your glory.

Do not hide your sensitivity away. Do not ignore your inner knowing to please someone else. Do not squash your deep feelings to fit in. You are not meant to fit in. You are meant to be you in all your incredible intensity. Honour your big, beautiful heart; your love; your wisdom; your truth. We do.

Forever and ever.

We love you,

Your Angels

Your Thoughts

Your Thoughts

About the Author

Anna Grace Taylor is an internationally known Angel Therapist, spiritual mentor, healer, singer and speaker. She has been featured on BBC Radio and Hay House Radio.

Using her natural intuitive gifts, developed by years of training and experience, Anna connects with Divine love and guidance to support people with all aspects of life and often acts as a catalyst for transformation for people all over the world.

Born eleven weeks prematurely and with cerebral palsy, Anna took her first independent steps at the age of six and learned to walk twice more following major surgery and long-term illness in her teens.

Currently living in England with her cat Rumi, she is a loving and compassionate woman with a remarkable ability to empathise and communicate – sharing her Daily Messages of Grace and Weekly Angel Reading videos with millions of people on social media.

Among her favourite things are live music, singing without an audience, long conversations, yummy food, warm sunshine and being an auntie to her amazing nieces and nephews.

www.annagracetaylor.com

Facebook: annataylormusicangel

Instagram: annagracetaylors

YouTube: annagracetaylors

Printed in Great Britain
by Amazon

53364704R00147